To Joan
Best wish
Marilyn

CW00601791

Fears, Tears, Cheers

One day my daughter said to me,
'I'd like to know of our family tree',
So I thought it would be good,
To start with tales of my childhood.
This book is the result of my journey,
To a time and place that once knew me.

Fears, Tears, Cheers

A 1950s Poetic Childhood

**written and illustrated by
M. B. CLARKSON**

First published in 2005 by
Marilyn B. Clarkson, 21 Dales Lane, Whitefield,
Greater Manchester, M45 7JN

© Marilyn B. Clarkson 2005

ISBN 0 9550526 0 2 *paperback*

The right of Marilyn B. Clarkson to be identified as the author of this work
has been asserted by her in accordance with the Copyright, Design and
Patents Act 1988.

All rights reserved. No part of this publication may be reproduced in any
material form (including photocopying or storing it in any medium by
electronic means and whether or not transiently or incidentally to some other
use of publication) without the written permission of the copyright owner
except in accordance with the provisions of the Copyright, Designs and
Patents Act 1988 or under the terms of a licence issued by the Copyright
Licensing Agency Ltd. 90 Tottenham Court Road, London, England W1P
9HE. Applications for the copyright owner's written permission to repro-
duce any part of this publication should be addressed to the publisher.

Produced by Freelance Publishing Services, Brinscall, Lancs
www.freelancepublishingservices.co.uk
Printed in Great Britain by Antony Rowe Ltd, Eastbourne

Contents

Acknowledgements

First and foremost my husband Tom. He threw down the gauntlet when he announced that my book would never materialize.

My family who gave me the extra encouragement that I did need.

Friends and colleagues, past and present, at St Mary's school, Prestwich, who endured my endless recitals.

Staff at Whitefield Library who came to my assistance when computing.

Tribute to Mother

When my childhood memories I sought,
I realised they were full of riches that couldn't be bought.
It must have been difficult, mother dear,
On your own, three girls to rear,
So thank you mother up above,
I always knew that I was loved.

Crockery

Cups, no saucers,
Plates mismatched,
Cutlery of different sizes,
Glasses chipped and cracked.

Washday Blues

Monday toil,
Clothes to boil,
To rid of soil.

The Look

Children with dirty faces,
Men looking tired and worn,
Women middle-aged at thirty,
In clothes all tattered and torn.

Back Yards

Tippler toilets,
Ash pits,
Metal bins,
No gardens to sit.

Grandma

Grandma liked to sit, in her rocking chair,
Cross her leg and swing her slippered foot in the air,
I would just sit and stare,
At the metal curlers in her hair.

Grandad

Grandad was a kindly man,
When I heard his knock, to the door I ran,
He always gave us sixpence each,
I used mine to buy some sweets,
He had a bristly chin,
That scratched and tickled my skin.

After we had eaten tea,
I liked to sit on Grandad's knee,
Watching as he lit his pipe,
Puffing and puffing until it went bright,
Long after he had gone,
The smell would linger on.

Teatime

Tablecloth set for tea,
Not meals balanced on your knee!

Wellies in the Snow

Did you ever go, for a walk in the snow,
And over the top of your wellies it did go?
Did you end up, with a chapped rim,
Where the top of your welly touched skin?

Where's Me Teddy!

I had a teddy bear, his name was Fred,
We often played together and he slept in my bed,
I'd brush his fur, make him smart,
And whisper that we'd never part.

One day I looked for him with care,
Under the bed and behind a chair,
'What's to do?' me mammy said,
'I've looked everywhere and can't find Fred'.

'Oh, is that all?
Teddy's are for children small,
Now that you are ten,
I've given him to little Ben!'

Donkey Derby

Sat in the saddle full of pride,
I was about to venture on my first donkey ride,
He was called Gentle Neddy,
And set off sedately when I was ready.

All of a sudden, with such force,
My donkey galloped like a racing horse,
I clung on grimly full of fear,
As he charged towards the pier.

Then just as quickly, he stopped stone dead,
I flew off and landed on my head,
What happened next, I can't decide,
But I never again wanted a donkey ride!

Next Door Neighbour

Mam fell out with the lady next door,
So my friend Julie, I could play with no more,
Then at last, they began to talk,
So Julie and I went for a walk.

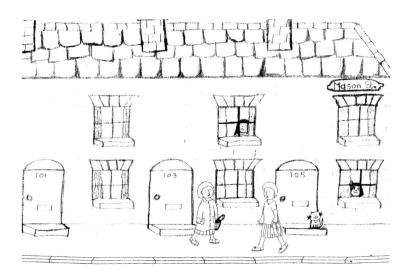

Donkey Stone

I liked to donkey-stone the step,
First I made it all wet,
Sometimes I would write my name,
Then I'd make it smooth again,
When I thought it looked right,
I left it to dry a creamy white.

Our Slide

It had been a frosty night,
The playground was covered, what a delight,
We took it in turn, to make a slide,
It went longer and shinier the more we glide,
It went very fast,
And looked like a river of glass.

The bell rang, school began,
Playtime came, we all ran,
Imagine how sad we felt,
The caretaker had covered it in salt!

Crusty Bread

'We need some more bread',
'I'll go', I said,
Off to the shop at the corner,
Inside it smelt all warm.

The lady in front bought some cheese,
My turn next, 'A large white crusty please',
I set off home, trying hard to resist,
Nibbling a corner all crunchy and crisp.

When I reached my front door,
The corners were no more!

Letter to Santa

Time to write our Christmas list,
Hoping we get all we wish,
In the post box it went?
No! Up the chimney it was sent!

Aunty Dorothy's

We're off to Aunty Dorothy's for a holiday,
We'll play with our cousins and have adventures every day,
They live in a pretty cottage, with a garden that is long,
Inside is a bathroom and a toilet that doesn't pong,
Rivers, streams, caves with residing bats,
Hadrian's Wall and fields with giant haystacks.

But first of all was an ordeal,
Because of the way it made me feel,
For on the coach to Carlisle,
We always had to stop awhile,
Whilst I got off quick,
As I was often sick!

Preventative Medicine

As children we didn't ail much at all,
Must have been all that malt and cod liver oil!

Barrow Bridge

Barrow Bridge here we come,
Let's go and have some fun,
Sixty-three steps, boating lake,
Swingboats and amusement arcade,
We only had our bus fare,
Did we really dare,
To put our pennies in the slot,
And watch the metal ball drop,
Flick the handle, watch it spin,
Praying and wishing that we'll win,
Did we win or did we lose?
Good job we were wearing our walking shoes!

The Middlebrook

As I set off for the Middlebrook, I made a little wish,
That this would be the day I would catch a fish,
I hadn't gone far,
With my jam jar,
When I saw my friend Jack,
He had a bucketful of fish and he gave me a stickleback.

Took home my new pet,
Mammy said, 'Leave it on the step',
Next time I looked, it wasn't swimming at all,
Clog wearing Annie had filled the jar with soil!

Pantomime

Mammy said, 'If you are good,
I will take you to see Red Riding Hood',
So of course we were,
She even bought us a chocolate bar.

Up the steps to reach the 'gods',
We took our seats, as the band warmed up,
The safety curtain was in place,
On it, an old man's smiling face.

When the curtain rose,
Dinky Dots appeared in pretty clothes,
They tap-danced in perfect rhythm,
Their hair and shoes adorned with ribbons,
They looked small and neat,
As they tip-tapped with their feet.

When the ghost came into view,
We all shouted, 'He's behind you!'
Then we had a sing-a-long,
Bunch of Coconuts was my favourite song.

We all booed at the villain,
Then cheered when the woodcutter killed him,
It was a night like no other,
We all thanked our mother,
When we went to The Grand,
To visit Pantoland.

School Dinners

School dinners were mostly good,
Even the thick gravy and the lumpy mashed spud,
No food on your plate could you leave,
Even if you began to heave.

Then one day in the middle of June,
Pudding was semolina and prunes,
No matter how hard I tried,
The prunes just wouldn't go inside.

The others cleaned and stacked their dishes,
Then they waited for me to finish,
I nudged my bowl away from me,
Then sat there shaking like a leaf on a tree.

A shadow loomed, the table shook,
As the dinner lady came to take a look,
'WHOSE IS THAT?' She shouted and frowned,
I froze with fear and my heart beat loud,
I am thankful to this day,
That my friends not a word did say.

The Fair Comes to Bolton

The fairground on a winter's night,
Was full of amazing sounds and sights,
The Waltzer went faster and faster,
Especially when it was pushed by the master,
The Big Wheel made me a scaredy cat,
You'd never get me on that!

Roll-a-Penny was good fun,
If some more pennies you won,
The sideshows looked very exciting,
Contortionists and boxers fighting,
Dances of the seven veils,
Creatures with two heads and tails!

The organ was mighty and grand,
With figures like a toytown band,
They shook their bells, tooted their flutes,
Triangles tinkled, they all looked cute,
Cymbals clashed, drums went wild,
People stood, watched and smiled.

When your fingers and toes began to freeze,
You could sit round a fire with a cupful of black peas.

Inside Out

Put my cardi' on inside out,
'Don't take it off!' my mammy did shout,
'It's bad luck', I heard her say,
'To put your cardi' the right way'.

Toys

We didn't have many toys,
But we could amuse ourselves for hours and hours,
The clothes maiden became a tent,
Or a shop with buttons to be spent,
But my favourite thing,
Was a phone made with cocoa tins and string!

Church

Sunday morning we went to church,
My sisters and I, on our seats did perch,
We would stand, kneel and pray,
We even sang the hymns that day.

I coughed, sneezed and made a din,
You couldn't miss Mass, it would be a sin!
The lady could no longer stand
The noise I was making with nose and hand.

On the shoulder she tapped me,
Then gave me her handkerchief,
On it was a pretty rose,
I thanked her and blew my nose.
It was only wet a bit,
But the kind lady let me keep it!

Baby in Pram

A pram outside a house did stand,
Sat a baby with rattle in hand,
Knocked and interrupted mum's talk,
'Can I take your baby for a walk?'
'Yes love, you may –
What's your name, by the way?'

Day Trip

Set off for Trinity Street Station,
Blackpool was our destination,
Mammy only got a small wage,
And our Jean was tall for her age,
She had to bend her knees,
As mammy said, 'One and three halves please'.

We were excited as we heard the tannoy announce,
The next train to arrive would be the Blackpool one,
As it slowed, we saw,
That it was a corridor.

In we got and shut the door,
We didn't want any more,
We fidgeted and made a fuss,
If anyone wanted to join us,
It usually worked like a dream,
But on reflection it was quite mean!

Beech Nut

Outside the shop on the wall,
Was a container that seemed very tall,
A penny in the slot, turn the knob,
Out came a beech nut to chew in your gob!

Sometimes I checked during the day,
If the arrow was pointing the right way,
When it was I knew what to do,
Instead of one out came two!

Circus

As the circus paraded through town,
I liked to watch the elephants and clowns,
Along Spa Road they went,
Into Queen's Park to pitch their tent.

Going to see it next week,
Can't wait to take a peek,
Big Night, Big Top,
Crisps and a bottle of pop!

Getting to your place was quite precarious,
The spaces beneath looked quite dangerous,
I always feared that I'd get trapped,
Or even fall through the gap!

What was lurking down below,
A tiger ready to eat me in one go?

Nitty Nora

Nitty Nora the bug explorer,
Discovered I had nits all o'er,
Gave me a card for all to see,
Then I saw it wasn't only me!

Hair was washed with derbac soap,
Fine toothcomb made it feel like rope,
Next time it was nice,
When she said 'No more lice!'

Put Something on your Feet!

Houses were very cold,
Warmed only by a fire of coal,
Gaps in doors and windows too,
Where the icy wind blew through,
Rag rugs on the flag floor,
A piece of carpet surrounded by lino.

That is why mammy insisted,
We always wore shoes or slippers,
She caught me in my bare feet,
Then let out a chilling shriek.

Being the baby, I didn't get shouted at much at all,
So when I did, I would bawl and bawl,
'Get out in the yard to stand,
Before you feel the back of my hand',
I went, and in the toilet stood,
My tears nearly caused a flood.

Sister Jean followed soon after,
That couldn't be the sound of laughter!
I can't remember her 'crime',
But she seemed to be having a good time,
Singing and dancing around,
In the snow that covered the ground!

Clogs

I wanted clogs so that I could skid,
Down the street like a dustbin lid,
Only for the poor children, I was told,
But how I longed for sparks from my soles.

Bus Fare

Dodging bus fares was a lark,
'Cept when you got caught,
Then you had to walk.

Cut Knee

I fell and cut my knee,
Then I hid behind a tree,
'Cos the lady said to me,
'That needs a stitch at the Infirmary!'

Coalman

When the coalman delivered our coal,
Mammy would inspect it as if it was gold,
One day she shouted, 'You can take that back,
I didn't order nutty slack!'

Orange Box

Dragged along the cobbles by my sister Jean,
I would sit in an orange box, feeling like a queen!

Market Stalls

The market stalls were a good place to play,
When everything had been cleared away,
We would jump from one to another,
Sometimes banging our heads on the cover!

Our Cat

We had a cat that liked to roam,
Far, far, far away from home,
When we wanted it to come in,
We would bang on a plate made of tin!

Julie's Hair

I always wanted long hair,
Just like the girl next door,
Put in rags every night,
Ringlets appeared, what a magical sight.

When mine grew below my ears,
Out came a pair of shears!

Bonfire Night

Bonfire Night is fast approaching,
Time to go a wood-poaching,
We store it in the air raid shelter,
This year's is going to be a belter.

Better get the Guy Fawkes ready,
It's really Olga's giant teddy,
Penny for the guy, Penny for the guy,
Then fireworks we can buy.

Bonfire is built in our back street,
Some of the neighbours bring out a seat,
It is lit by the man next door,
Soon the flames begin to soar.

Potatoes are put in the fire to bake,
They won't take long, we can't wait.
Colours and crackles fill the night,
Snowstorms and sparklers are my favourite sight,
Dodging jack jumpers and bangers,
Thrown by the local gangs.

Potatoes must be ready to eat,
Taking care of the heat,
Looking like lumps of coal,
Fingers burnt as you got hold,
They tasted ever so good,
Even though they were hard as wood!

The Slipper Baths

When I went to High Street Baths, it wasn't for a swim,
I was given a towel and soap and shown where to go in.
The room seemed enormous, the bath was too,
I couldn't see any taps, what would I do?

All of a sudden from behind the wall, the water did flow,
When to stop it, when it was full, how did they know?
I clambered in, I could have had a swim,
The water went way past my chin.

I slipped and slid as I got out,
That's why they named them slipper baths, no doubt,
Dangers were unforeseen,
For a child to be clean!

Dentist

Going to the dentist was a scary affair,
When you sat in that big black chair,
A mask came slowly to your face,
'Just breathe and you'll have dreams of a lovely place',
The gas smelled horrid, the dream was too,
I was in a dark tunnel without a view,
Then appeared rattling bones, skeletons,
And the sound of moans,
When I awoke my tooth I could see,
My tongue felt a hole where it used to be.

The Party

It was Jennie's seventh birthday one Saturday in May,
Party food, big balloons and many games to play.
The fun would begin at quarter to four,
I was so excited, I'd never been to a party before,
Mammy put on my best frock,
For a present a pair of socks.

I set off on my own,
To find Jennie's home,
At last I found her garden gate,
Went up the steps to knock and wait,
From within I could hear the noise,
Of excited girls and boys.

Feeling shy and all alone,
I turned around and sloped off home.
Mammy was cross, she angrily said,
'Instead of that present, I could have bought some bread!'

Lonely Boy

There was a boy who lived down our street,
He always wore wellies on his feet,
His jumper was matted and small,
He never wiped his nose at all,
He was always on his own,
So I said to my friend Joan,
'Shall we go and play with him?'
'No, I've not to play with Jim',
I felt sorry for him that day,
So I asked if he wanted to play,
'Yes', he said, 'If you do not squirm',
'When I eat a juicy worm!'

May Sunday

Every girl wanted to be May Queen,
Or a trainbearer, would be a dream.
Today we find out who it will be,
I said a little prayer and hoped it would be me.

Adrienne Stone would wear the crown,
One of the trainbearers was Anne Brown,
Pauline and I weren't too sad,
We liked Adrienne, so we told her we were glad.

Adrienne practised crowning that day,
While we sang 'Queen of the May'.
The weeks passed,
May Sunday at last.

Adrienne looked lovely with her staff and crown,
A long satin train and a jewel encrusted gown.
The band played, the Walks began,
I quickly waved to Mam and Gran.

I felt good and looked my best,
With my veil and headdress,
My frock was white and lacey,
Made by my Auntie Elsie,
Black patent ankle straps,
People clapped as we walked past.

Saturday Cinema

Off to the Windsor on a Saturday Morn,
To watch the films, but no popcorn,
The cartoons were very funny,
Mickey Mouse and Bugs Bunny,
The Three Stooges were a riot,
They prodded, poked and were never quiet.

Flash Gordon and Superman,
Always escaped and the baddies ran,
Sometimes the film broke down,
We would stamp our feet, boo and frown.
I liked Tarzan best,
When we all pounded our chest.

If a western had been shown,
I would gallop all the way home.

First Day of School

My first day of school is very clear,
I had to leave my mammy dear,
I cried and cried, but Mrs Hare,
Made me stand upon a chair.

Queen's Park

Queen's Park was our second home,
We went with friends or on our own,
Sometimes we would feed the ducks,
Or just run around the 'pie crust',
You could have enormous fun,
Playing hide and seek amongst the rhodendron.

The paddling pool wasn't very clean,
Broken glass couldn't be seen,
Mud would ooze between your toes,
You sometimes had to hold your nose,
There was even a shop,
Where you could buy sweets and pop.

The swings and slide were always busy,
The witch's hat made you very dizzy,
My favourite was of course,
Sat at the front of the rocking horse.

Moss Bank Park

Moss Bank Park was a bus ride away,
The sandpit was a good place to play,
In the playground, lots of choice,
Then to see the birds that made lots of noise!

The rock gardens were a child's paradise,
Some things were shrunken in size,
Miniature waterfalls and streams,
Hidden by shrubs and trees.

I was especially fond,
Of the goldfish in the pond,
You could go around and around,
Never covering the same ground,
Once I found a lovely place to sit,
Next time I looked, I couldn't find it!
Stepping stones, pine cones,
Hiding from Jean and Joan,
If you got caught running about,
The park keeper would shout,
'Oi you lot, get out!'

Bathing Hat

How I hated my bathing hat,
It had to be worn, no doubt about that!
Pulled on tight, hair pushed in,
My eyebrows nearly touched my chin.

When I removed it, how I did yelp,
It felt as though I was being scalped.

Knock a Door

Knock a door run,
Was lots of fun.